NORTH MIDLAND

Portrait of a Famous Route

BOB PIXTON

Derby's first station, exterior, 1840.

RUNPAST PUBLISHING

Published by Runpast Publishing,
10 Kingscote Grove, Cheltenham, Gloucestershire GL51 6JX

Typesetting and reproduction by Viners Wood Associates – 01452 812813
Printed in England by The Amadeus Press Ltd., Cleckheaton

ISBN 1 870754 47 6

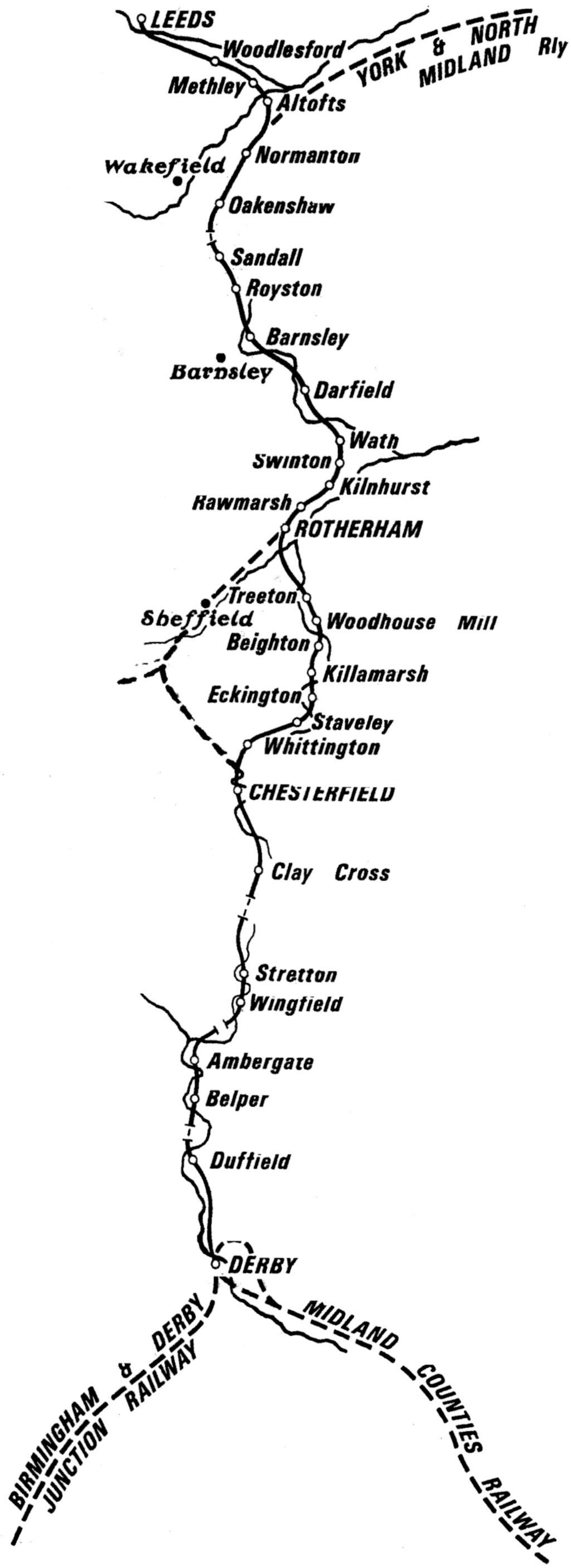

Map of the North Midland Railway route from Derby to Leeds, opened throughout in 1840, along with early main line connections, including the Sheffield and Rotherham Railway, and the Midland Railway line of 1870 from Chesterfield to Sheffield.

Detailed maps in the book cover Derby, Ambergate, Avenue Sidings and Chesterfield in late Midland Railway days.

Leaving Derby, 20 May 1950. Passing Derby Station North box and the magnificent signal gantry is this local passenger train, which will travel along the North Midland route to Chesterfield, before taking the 1870 Midland Railway line into Sheffield. Midland 2P 4-4-0 No.40472 from Hasland shed (code 18C), with 'LMS' still on its tender, is in charge. Having set off from platform 3 it is about to switch onto the down main line.

R J Buckley, Initial Photographics

Foreword

Waiting outside the New Inn on King Street, Derby in early 1835 were four horses and a yellow carriage. Climbing aboard was George Stephenson and his Secretary, Charles Binns, on their way to survey the best railway route between Derby and Leeds. The one chosen was, in the eyes of the surveyors, capable of being worked by the steam locomotives of the time. It also compromised between the capital needed to deviate through centres of population and the extra revenue that would be generated. The line followed the contours offered by the valleys made by the Rivers Derwent, Amber, Rother, Don, Dearne, Calder and Aire. The wishes of the promoters also had to be taken into consideration. They saw money to be made in the transport of minerals; the movement of people was lower down their list of priorities. Large radii curves and shallow gradients were to be hallmarks of the construction, although it would be some years before the speeds attained benefitted from this policy. By a combination of these factors the line avoided Sheffield, as gradients of 1 in 100 and a long tunnel would have been necessary for an approach from the south. The North Midland Railway started operations from Derby to Chesterfield and Masborough (Rotherham) on 11 May 1840. The Sheffield and Rotherham Railway provided a line between those two places, opened on 31 October 1838. (It was another thirty years before the Midland Railway's direct line from Chesterfield to Sheffield opened, on 1 February 1870.) Wakefield did not want this new-fangled railway and Castleford was too far east, so the line went between the two!

But the 72 miles-long line, opened throughout from Derby to Leeds from 1 July 1840, was still a massive undertaking; it had 200 bridges and seven tunnels and cost over £3.3million.

The railway's first locomotives were 2-2-2s which ran the passenger and mail trains, while 0-4-2s were constructed to haul goods traffic.

Along with the Midland Counties and the Birmingham and Derby Junction Railways, the North Midland became an integral part of the Midland Railway when it was incorporated on 10 May 1844. With the three railways all running to Derby, it was the natural place to locate the headquarters of the Midland, growing over the years to include the famous locomotive factory, as well as rolling stock and signal works. Rixon Bucknall stated in his book *Our Railway History* that the Midland 'had begun as an island, surrounded by other and powerful systems, but it developed its cross-country services and through connections until they ... had become the backbone of the railway map of England' and the North Midland route formed a vital part of that backbone.

The North Midland Railway is noted for its particularly fine station houses, designed by Francis Thompson, whilst even the tunnel portals at Clay Cross boast ornamental stone work. The excavations for this tunnel exposed a lot of mineral wealth just waiting to be exploited, which it duly was by, amongst others, George Stephenson, leading to the formation of the famous Clay Cross Company. In 1845, the first rail-borne coal to arrive in London came from Clay Cross and over the years vast quantities of coal have travelled along the North Midland route.

Acknowledgements

The idea for this project came from a discussion with Stephen Mourton of Runpast in 1998 and without whose help it would not have matured into a three volume pictorial book. There are local people along the route, whose involvement has enriched the account, these include: Graham Perrin; Robert Gratton; Glynn Waite; and members of Chesterfield Local History Society.

Public libraries have been a great source of information, especially the local studies sections at Chesterfield, Sheffield and Leeds. Various societies have also been a source of encouragement, including the Midland Railway, Signalling Record, Engine Shed, London & North Western, Lancashire & Yorkshire, Great Central, Railway & Canal Historical and Railway Correspondence & Travel, also the Midland Railway Trust and Roger Carpenter. Unfortunately a section on Avenue Coking Plant wasn't able to be included in spite of the help given by many local people and workers from the plant.

Photographic credits, as far as it is possible to tell, have been appended to the appropriate captions.

Part One
Derby to Chesterfield

Contents

Introduction

The whole of the original North Midland Railway line between Derby and Chesterfield is still open, although it has been subject to expansion and contraction at various times. With the construction of Clay Cross tunnel, rich seams of coal were discovered and the firm of George Stephenson and Co was set up to look after the mining interests. Local deposits of iron and limestone led eventually to the Clay Cross Co being formed. George Stephenson himself rented Tapton House, near Chesterfield, to oversee not only the construction of the railway, but also the profitable mining concerns. Blast furnaces were erected in 1846 and so the personal fortune of Stephenson was secured, as well as the prestige earned from his railway ventures. When he died in 1848, the whole of Chesterfield closed for the day of his funeral.

The development of a line west from Ambergate to penetrate the LNWR strongholds of Lancashire and Cheshire also produced a route to London from, in particular, Manchester and enabled the eventual owners, the Midland Railway, to become partners in the Cheshire Lines, extending to the Liverpool area. With the development of a line along the Erewash valley to Trent, a very busy railway carrying vast quantities of coal to the south was established.

Derby Station

In the early 1830s, three companies were jostling to establish a presence in Derby, each from a different direction. At a Town Hall meeting in December 1835, chaired by the Mayor, public approval was given for two of the companies – the North Midland, with its proposed line to Leeds, and the Birmingham & Derby Junction Railway – to meet head on rather than in separate termini. As the third company – the Midland Counties Railway from Leicester and Nottingham – also had a proposal for a terminus, the Town Council suggested a joint through station for them all on land adjacent to the River Derwent at The Holmes. Due to susceptibility to flooding, the companies preferred a smaller site nearer the town centre on Castle Fields, though this would be a terminus. In June 1838 the Council agreed to make better road provision to The Holmes site and the next year plans were published for a station to serve all three companies, as well as workshops and engine shed for each. In April 1839, tenders were invited, with Thomas Jackson of London being awarded the just under £40,000 contract. The North Midland Railway was the lead company for the project with the other two paying just under £5,000 each as well as 6% per annum for their share of the accomodation. The building consisted of a fine two-storey stone block flanked by windowed walls. The through station opening in 1840, and, apart from modifications, survived until the early 1950s internal rebuilding and the 1980s external 'modernisation'.

Derby's first station, north end, 1840. The station consisted of a single platform, over 1,000 feet long with a protruding central section. This enabled each company to have a part and to operate it independently of the others. Facing passengers on the platform were three 34' train sheds covering the through tracks and numerous small turntables. Of the three lines to share the station, the NMR was the last to operate, from 11 May 1840 as far as Masborough, across the river from Rotherham. This town had been linked with Sheffield for almost 18 months since 31 October 1838. The 'Great Midland Amalgamation Bill' brought all three companies under the directorship of George Hudson four years later.

The North Midland, like many large employers, found that it made sense to build houses for its workforce – 57 terraced homes on Calvert Street (used to be North Street), Midland Terrace and Place in 1841/2. These, like the ones in Swindon and Crewe, are now 'Conservation Areas'. A Club and Institute was erected by the MR in 1894.

Above: Robert Stephenson & Co. supplied 2-2-2 locomotives for the North Midland Railway.

SHEFFIELD TELEGRAPH
ARRIVAL
CARRIAGE EXIT
DEPARTURE

Left, above: Derby station, exterior, 1891. Improvements to the facilities started in the early 1850s and consisted of a booking hall, 1st class refreshment rooms and separate waiting rooms for Ladies and Gentlemen, as well as some offices for the officials of the Midland Railway. In the basement a 2nd class refreshment room was built along with stores for wine and provisions and a kitchen. In 1857 a two-storey stone building was added to the right hand side of the main building: this was for the use of shareholders. Over the next year, a similar block was erected to the east of the main entrance to keep a symmetrical look. Between the two blocks a pillared wall was put up through which carriages passed dropping off and picking up passengers. *Author's collection*

Left, below: Derby station, exterior, circa 1910. In 1893 the station buildings were the subject of further alterations. The covered way for carriages dating from the 1850s was dismantled and in its place a new two storey block put up in front of the original buildings, stretching from the shareholder's wing to the wing on the left. Decorative domed towers were added at the ends of the central block, surrounded by decorated stone and a clock. There were offices on the first floor and different class booking offices and arrival halls.

A glass covered arrival and departure area was built in front using much of the material from the earlier construction. *Stations UK*

Above: Derby station, exterior, 1954. This view, further to the right of the previous pictures, includes the covered way which linked the station to the Midland Hotel, a speculative venture by Francis Thompson, once privately owned, but bought by the MR in 1860 for £10,050. It consisted of an 'H' shape, with accomodation being on two, three-storey arms with a single connecting block containing the entrance hall. Alterations including wings in 1872 and 1888, increasing the height of the connecting block, and more recently, a new entrance and porch. In 1991, further extensions maintained the Midland as Derby's leading hotel.

Regrettably, the old station buildings were demolished and replaced by a modern structure opening in stages from 1986. *Author's collection*

Due to overcrowding and general difficulty in working the station, a 'Derby Station Improvements Committee' was set up in 1858. It recommended spending £2,000 on the removal of the turntables, alterations to the platform, the building of an island platform and a connecting staircase. Thus platforms 1, 2 and 3 as we know them today were born. Demand outstripped supply in the 1870s. Consequently, another island platform was built - platforms 4 & 6 - with a bay - 5 - at the Birmingham end. At this point, the station protruded beyond the original train shed and so an awning was built for platform 6 to ensure all portions were under cover, passenger comfort was very important in those competitive days. These alterations opened just in time for the Royal Agricultural Show held in Derby in June 1871. A new refreshment room was built on this new island and a staircase connected all the platforms together. The station also had other refreshment and dining rooms to cater for passengers on long journeys, who often had to change trains at Derby.

Above: Derby station, interior, 1911. A train stands at platform 2. The signals controlling the crossover have been specially altered to suit the situation by having the pivot half way along the arm and not close to one end. *Author's collection*

Below: Derby station, interior, 1953. To the left of the scissors crossover and the colour light signals is the controlling signal box, Station 'A', it also controlled the scissors crossover between platforms 3 & 4. Even at that time there were plenty of gaps in the station's roof. In the following year, the station's rebuilding did away with the train shed. *Stations UK*

S TO S

674
614

Left, above: Derby station, circa 1890. Looking north from platform 4 shows a lot of activity. Under the long train shed over platform 1, the original single platform, are a set of 'plum & spilt milk' carriages of the L&NWR. On lines serving platforms 2,3 & 4 are the 2-4-0 engines that pulled fast trains of the day. Along with the gas light, the signals are worthy of a second look. On the back of one is clearly written '3 TO S', the one to its left has '3 TO W'. These indicated either the route to Birmingham (south) or to Trent (west): they are arranged in order of height not in strict geographical layout.

R S Carpenter collection

Left, below: Derby station, circa 1912, departure for Burton. A fine picture of a Midland 'Spinner'. The development of steam sanding gear by the Works Manager at Derby, Francis Holt, improved the adhesion of single-wheelers, leading to a revival of the type by the Midland Railway in the late 1880s. Johnson built his first in 1887 and no less than 95, of various classes, were built over a fourteen year period. The '115' class, built in the 1890s, are regarded as probably the finest and most successful of all the Midland bogie singles. The one pictured here was No.119 prior to the 1907 renumbering scheme, then becoming No.674, and was withdrawn in April 1925. Another member of the class, No.118/673, is preserved and belongs to the National Railway Museum.

An interesting set of coaches on the train, the second vehicle appears to be a six-wheel van. On the left is the ticket platform. Before stations were 'closed', trains stopped just outside and tickets were examined, after which the train went into the station. This one, London Road, closed in 1900. For trains coming in from the North Midland line, there had been Derwent Bridge Ticket Platform, which closed in 1892.

R S Carpenter collection

Above: Derby station, June 1929. Midland engines did not have a monopoly here. Ex-L&NWR 'Experiment' class 4-6-0 No.5508 *Buckland* waits at platform 3 with a train, probably bound for Derby's erstwhile rival town in the locomotive building world, Crewe, via Stoke-on-Trent. Indeed, there had been an LNWR engine shed in Derby, closed soon after the grouping. *RAS Marketing*

40472

Left: Derby station, April 1952. Although being an important railhead, with the Works turned over to the war effort, Derby had very few air raids in World War 2. However, the station did suffer a direct hit on 15 January 1941; six people were killed and eight injured. A large portion of platform 6, including its roof and footbridge, was destroyed. Two weeks later the station was almost back to normal. In 1952 a £200,000 modernisation plan was unveiled. This involved the removal of the crumbling, dark train sheds and the erection of individual roofs on each platform: these would be new, clean and let in plenty of light. New refreshment rooms were to be built on platforms 1 and 4/6. A new footbridge was to connect all the platforms. Given the end of rationing the year before and the desire in the country for a new post-war direction, these changes were seized upon eagerly. The old stone exterior was retained though. This view from the works footbridge shows a hive of activity. Station pilot is 4-4-0 No.40472 while Class Five 4-6-0 No.44776 is at the head of a train at platform 6. Sister engine No.45145 is at platform 2 ready to depart from the southern end of the station. While the interior under the roof looks gloomy, there is some welcome light around the footbridge.

Frank Ashley

Above: Derby station, 23 May 1954. This view north from the Works footbridge shows the station in the throes of rebuilding: the large, dark overall roof was replaced by a lower, more open one. Basically, the roof supports consisted of two 'T' pieces of reinforced concrete projecting from the platform. The roof went across the top, and, underneath, was space for buildings such as the buffet, waiting rooms and toilets. Almost 30 years later, some further work was done to the roof. A new footbridge linking the platforms is also being built. The lines to the right include the paired goods lines which effectively bypassed the station.

E R Morten

5628

45660

Left, above: Derby, 1948. Resplendent in the May sunshine in red livery is Crewe-built 'Jubilee' class 4-6-0 No.5628 *Somaliland*, much to the delight of the young schoolboy, probably now retired! The photo illustrates an activity that was interesting to watch if done correctly, and, if not, watch out! Using one of the water columns on the platform, a flexible leather bag was put into the opening in the 3,500 gallon capacity tender. A wheel on the column controlled the flow of water. When sufficient water had passed, then the hose was removed after the tap had been turned off – to the delight of trainspotters, sometimes the order was reversed and those too slow to get out of the way got a little wet! The engine received its BR number, by adding 40000, in December; it had almost thirteen more years life left before withdrawal. *Midland Railway Trust*

Left, below: Derby, 1950. Platform 4 at around 10.30 on 2 June sees the arrival of the Bristol train that set off almost three hours previously from Bradford, hauled by Bristol Barrow Road 'Jubilee' 4-6-0 No.45660 *Rooke*. At platform 2 is a northbound train headed by a Compound 4-4-0, still with its previous owner's initials on the tender. At this end the roof was little more than a set of metal girders in the air offering no protection whatsoever to passengers. *H C Casserley*

Above: Derby, 1963. The rebuilding of the roof is now complete. The concrete that is now 'Main Line' green supports the flat roofs and the whole station has a wide, open feel about it. The water column, and on the adjacent platform, a set of corridor end connections are still throwbacks to the pre-war days. The locomotive, No.45685 *Barfleur*, is another Barrow Road engine. Dieselisation had taken a strong hold by this time, as a result of which *Barfleur* was one of the depleted number of 'Jubilees' at Bristol available for cross-country services from the West Country and South Wales to the north-east. *Stations UK*

The mid-day train to London. Post-war was a time of great experimentation on BR, and three different prototype main-line diesels are illustrated on this working, which left Manchester at 10.0am and Derby at 12.5pm. The timetable shows a journey time from Derby to St. Pancras of 205 minutes for the 128 miles, with stops at Loughborough, Leicester, Market Harborough, Kettering, Wellingborough, Bedford and Luton.

Left, above: Derby, 1949. Although the quality of this picture is below standard, it is included for its historical interest. The diesel-electric engines, 10000 and 10001, were built here under the direction of Chief Mechanical Engineer, H G Ivatt, as he tried to keep abreast of technological developments. Only the first was finished in LMS days (just) and had the letters LMS on its side.

R J Buckley, Initial Photographics

Left, below: Derby, 1951. Regular passengers on the train to the capital had the excitement of new types of motive power. On 9 January it was the job of the Ashford-built Southern Region diesel No.10201.

Author's collection

Above: Derby, 1952. 'Fell' diesel-mechanical engine No.10100 was being tried on the Manchester to London route. This was its first express run, on 10 March. It is a matter of speculation as to the discussions going on with the passengers and officials around the MR water column at the south end of the platform. They would surely have found it difficult to believe that nearly 50 years later, a train at a similar time, one of the regular hourly departures to London, does the journey in just over half the time taken in 1952.

R J Buckley, Initial Photographics

Above: Derby, 1951. Displacement of D16/2 4-4-0s from their previous haunts by BR Standard locos led to them being used on different services, such as Lincoln and Nottingham to Derby trains. However, before they could be used, the route had to be checked to ensure that there were sufficient clearances and the engines wouldn't derail, and at what speeds they should undertake manoeuvres. At just after 9.30 on 13 April, No.62590 is using the scissors crossover, anxiously watched by officials. *T G Wassell*

Below: Arriving at Derby, 1955. The busy railway station's unnatural peace is shattered by the arrival of No.20 Strike Special train from Leeds to St Pancras behind 'Jubilee' 4-6-0 No.45608 *Gibraltar* on 2 June. The railwaymen's strike at the time reflected the discontent of long serving skilled workers finding that their pay and conditions in a rapidly changing post-war Britain lagged behind unskilled workers in newer industries. *R J Buckley, Initial Photographics*

Above: Southbound departure, Derby, 1960. Leaving platform 6 with a train that had originated in the NE region is 'Jubilee' 4-6-0 No.45572 *Eire*, bound for the south. London Road Junction box, shown here, was a large cabin with 83 levers, lasting until 1969 when it was superseded by the power control cabin a stone's throw away on the down side of the Trent line. Opposite this box was a milepost with '0' miles (from Derby) on it. *Midland Railway Trust*

Below: Derby, arrival from Nottingham. Looking south from the Holland Street works footbridge shows London Road Junction in the early 1960s. The train from Nottingham is curving its way onto the down passenger line and about to enter the station. Fairburn 2-6-4T No.42053 is pulling the long train. Passing under the bridge to the rear are the lines to Birmingham, while those to the right go to the ex-L&NWR/North Staffordshire joint goods shed.
Author's collection

To allow for uninterrupted working of passenger trains, the goods lines bypassed the station to the east.
Above: Derby, 1930s. Heading north along the down goods is LMS 0-6-0 No.4015 with quite a mixture of loose coupled open wagons, typical of the day. To the rear are the signals of Station North box, which is on the right, while under the gantry on the left is Engine Sidings No.1 box controlling the northern entry to the shed and locomotive works. *Author's collection*

Below: Derby, 1954. Photographed from the northern footbridge is Stanier 2-8-0 No.48070 (complete with snow plough) hauling a northbound freight, while a trip working is on the left. Steps to platform six are in the course of construction from the covered footbridge. *R S Carpenter collection*

Above: Derby Station North box, interior. Some of the 60 levers in the box have been pulled to the 'off' position and so are allowing train movements while most are in the 'on' position with the signals and points being set against movement. *R K Blencowe collection*

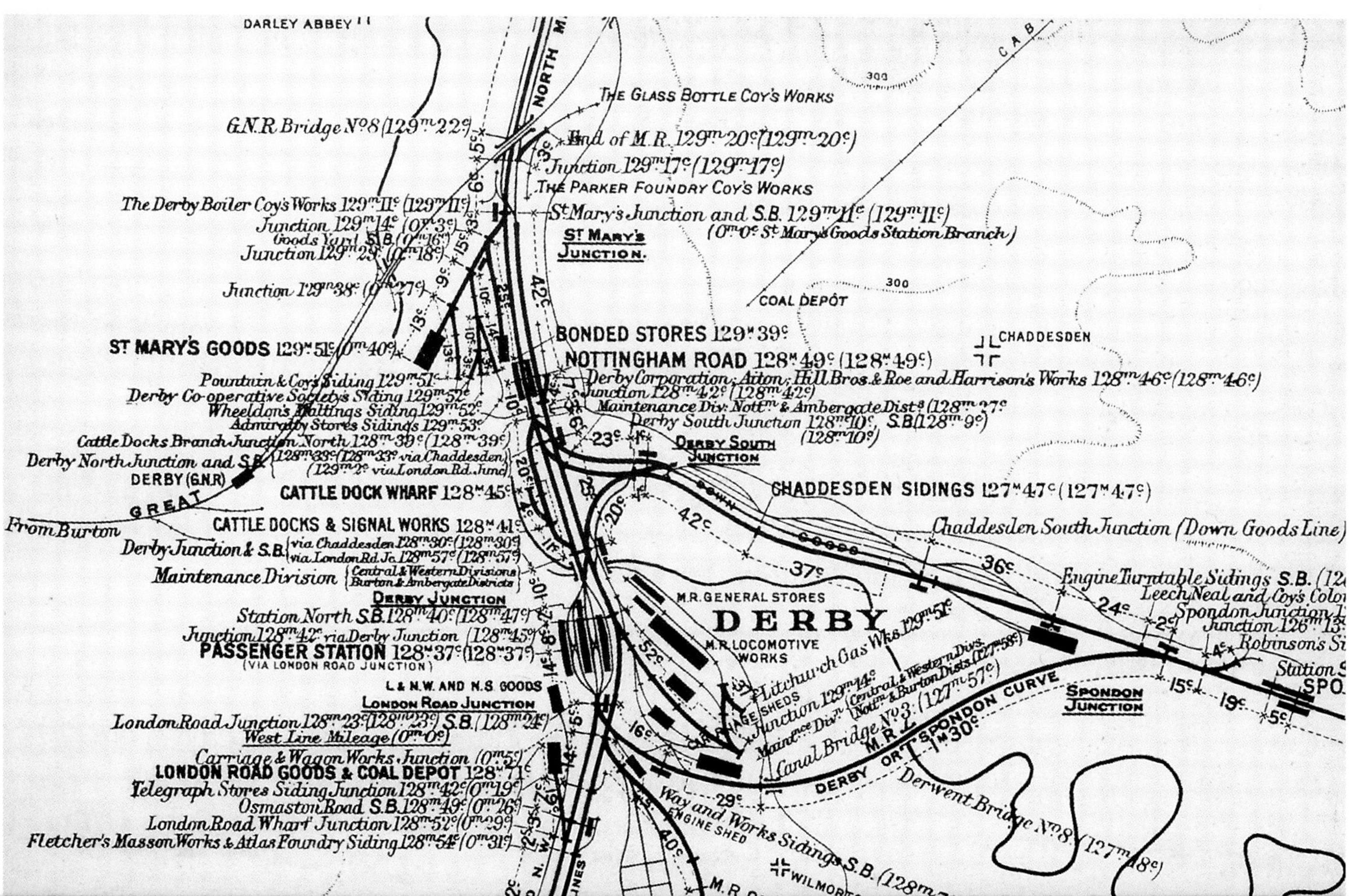

Above: Ex-North Midland Railway engine shed, 1920. All three railway companies that converged on Derby built their own shed and workshops. Both the Birmingham & Derby and the Midland Counties Railway built three road brick engine sheds. The former's was at the south end and was demolished after about 30 years use. The latter's was at the north end of the station, and after it ceased to be used for its original purpose, became the shareholders meeting place. It was the NMR's establishment that was enlarged to become Derby Works. The Thompson designed shed had 16 roads, each capable of holding two engines, and was polygonal in design with a central turntable. The pointed roof top was 48'10" high. Adjacent to this roundhouse were the NMR's main workshops in the shape of the letter 'V' with the engine shed in the apex. Next to the NMR's workshops was that of the MCR comprising an engine workshop and a machine shop. Another similar roundhouse opened in 1847 and a larger, 24 road shed in 1852. No. 4 shed opened in 1890 as part of a double structure – the other half was never built. Instead a 60' turntable was put in its place in 1900. Many years later, this became the site of Etches Park diesel depot. No.1 shed became part of the works and was used for engine repairs. It was the arrival of Matthew Kirtley in 1844 that brought order and standardisation to the separate companies that had merged to form the Midland Railway earlier that year. As trains were becoming heavier, engines were too light to haul them, hence his programme for the development of 0-6-0 engines to be not only repaired at Derby, but also to be built there (from 1851) and so reduce dependency on outside manufacturers. The MR coded the shed No.1, which changed to 17A in 1935 when it was home to around 100 engines. By the late 1950s this had increased by half again, eventually it closed to steam in March 1967, coded 16C in its last four years. *H C Casserley*

Right, above: A study in tanks, 9 August 1920. On the right is 0-4-0ST no.1514 dating from 1897, used for shunting around sharp curves in workshops and factories. In 1930 it was sold to Pentrich Colliery, near Derby. On the left is Kirtley outside framed 0-6-0WT No.1604 built in 1862, specially designed as a banking engine on the Lickey incline, which it did until 1883. It was withdrawn in 1928. Note the primitive protection for the footplate crews. This view was taken from the station with No.1 shed just off to the right: the building seen here is the coaling shed. With the construction of No.4 shed in 1890, a new double coaling stage was opened, while in 1936 the LMS erected a modern two-road concrete mechanical coaling plant. *H C Casserley*

Right, below: Prominent is Johnson 1P 0-4-4T No. 1429, which survived into the BR era as No.58090. The other tank locomotive in the picture, a Deeley 3P 0-6-4T, was not so fortunate; the whole class of forty was withdrawn between 1935 and 1938. Johnson 4-4-0 No. 502 was built in 1897 and lasted until 1961, often being used to haul Royal trains. Eighteen foot above the floor the longitudinal steel girders that supported the roof are evident in this view as are the smoke hoods. These were only at the centre of the radiating roads and so the engines had to be correctly positioned. *H C Casserley*

1804
1514

1429

The shape of the future, 20 July 1935. Derby has a long history of experimenting with diesel power. A Johnson 0-6-0T, No.1831, was completely rebuilt in 1932 as the diesel engine shown here. The experiences gleaned from this and others resulted in the LMS Traffic Committee authorising the purchase of twenty 350hp 0-6-0 diesel-electric shunting engines in the very month this picture was taken. A variation of the design became the standard BR shunter. Standing alongside it is ex-MR 4-4-0 No.459.
H C Casserley

Derby Junction, 1930s. 4-4-0 No.736, a Johnson 3P rebuilt by Fowler, heads an express from the north into Derby station across the 'Five Arches' bridge. This bridge over the River Derwent was a serious traffic bottleneck for over fifty years. Even though four tracks approached it from the south, only two lines actually crossed the river. In 1892 two more lines were added as well as connections to the loco works and a bridge over the Derby Canal too, all for £15,863. A fine gantry of lower quadrant signals controls the main line here, note that black chevrons haven't yet replaced black vertical stripes, which in turn replaced a black horizontal stripe in 1911, on the back of distant signals. Home signals had a black circle on the reverse until 1906.

Author's collection

Above: Derby Junction, 2 September 1958. The 5.48pm for Nottingham, whose engine is ex-LNER 'A5' class 4-6-2T No.69816, has just left Derby station and is crossing the Five Arches bridge. At the junction a short distance ahead, it will swing east, via Chaddesden, and will travel along the original Midland Counties Railway route between the two towns. Stops along the way will be Spondon, Borrowash, Draycott & Breaston, Sawley Junction, Trent, Attenborough and Beeston, taking 49 minutes. For well over 25 years after opening, trains along the former Midland Counties line from Nottingham had a difficulty if they wanted to proceed north after stopping at Derby station: they were facing the wrong way! They would pass Spondon station, go north and then swing west to arrive at the north end of Derby station. In 1867 a short (almost 2 miles) curve was built that allowed these trains to enter the station from the south. This 'Spondon Curve' went from west of the station there, over the river and then the canal on a swing bridge, to arrive at London Road Junction, south of Derby station. *R J Buckley, Initial Photographics*

Below: Derby Junction, looking north, 1960. At the northern end of the 'Five Arches' over the River Derwent was the departure of the line east to Nottingham from the main line. Controlling events until 1969 was this typical MR wooden box containing 52 levers in a tumbler frame. The facing signals are, from the left: down main, down goods, up Chaddesden and the bi-directional Independent line and its link to the up Chaddesden. The up signals, of which only the black and white backs show here, are, from the left: up main, up goods and the crossover to the up main. The pair on the right control the Independent line and its connection to the up goods.
R K Blencowe collection

Above: Derby Junction, 1951. On its way with empty carriage stock from Chaddesden to Derby station is Ivatt 2-6-0 No.43048, complete with a double chimney that would soon be replaced by the single variety.

R J Buckley, Initial Photographics

Below: Derby South Junction, 12 July 1951. To avoid reversals in Derby station and to allow trains for the Trent direction to bypass the station, a short – 23chains – curve was built. This left the main line at Derby North Junction and went east to meet the line from Trent at Derby South Junction, which is the box shown here. Ex-MR Johnson 0-6-0 No.58125 is passing on its way to Chaddesden sidings. Although it is some three years since nationalisation, the engine still has traces of its LMS ownership on the tender, while the third wagon still appears to belong to the Great Western! The lines south to Derby Junction and north to North Junction were controlled by means of this magnificent signal gantry. The two chief routes would be along the main and goods towards North Junction as indicated by the higher of the posts, making them stand out. *R J Buckley, Initial Photographics*

Passenger trains between Derby and Chesterfield from the LMS time table dated October 1st 1934

(Trains travelling a shorter distance, i.e. Derby - Ambergate or Clay Cross - Chesterfield are not shown)

Weekday service

				MX	MX					SX		
Derby	dep.	12.12	12.28	3.10	5.50	6.20	7.48	8.15	8.46	9.50	10.3	11.17
Derby, Nottingham Road												
Duffield						6.32	7.58		8.57		10.13	
Belper						6.41	8.4		9.4			
Ambergate						6.50	8.10		9.12		10.24	
Wingfield						7.1			9.20			
Stretton (for Ashover)						7.12			9.28			
Clay Cross						7.21			9.34			
Chesterfield	arr.		1.6	3.58	6.25	7.28	8.29		9.40	10.13	10.44	
Chesterfield	dep.		1.10	4.2	6.31	7.34	8.32			10.15	10.48	
Sheffield	arr.	1.5		4.23	6.52	8.17	8.56	9.7		10.33	11.10	12./ 5

Weekday service

Derby	dep.	12./ 45	1./ 41	3./ 33	5./ 35	6./ 55	8./ 9	9./ 45	11./ 12
Derby, Nottingham Road									
Duffield						7./ 6		9./ 56	
Belper						7./ 14		10./ 2	
Ambergate						7./ 22		10./ 8	
Wingfield						7./ 30		10./ 16	
Stretton (for Ashover)						7./ 38		10./ 24	
Clay Cross						7./ 44		10./ 30	
Chesterfield	arr.	1./ 20		4./ 5	6./ 11	7./ 50	8./ 39	10./ 36	
Chesterfield	dep.	1./ 22		4./ 7	6./ 13	7./ 52	8./ 42	10./ 38	
Sheffield	arr.	1./ 45	2./ 32	4./ 26	6./ 34	8./ 13	9./ 3	11./ 12	12.10

12.44	a.m. trains
11./ 45	p.m. trains
MX	Mondays excepted
SX	Saturdays excepted

Sunday service

Derby	dep.	12.12	12.28	3.10	6.50	11.15	1./ 35	5./ 42	6./ 30	6./ 55	9./ 20	11./ 12
Derby, Nottingham Road												
Duffield					7.1				6./ 39		9./ 30	
Belper					7.10				6./ 47		9./ 37	
Ambergate					7.21				6./ 55	7./ 12	9./ 44	
Wingfield					7.34					7./ 20		
Stretton (for Ashover)					7.46					7./ 28		
Clay Cross					7.52					7./ 34		
Chesterfield	arr.		1.6	3.58	7.59	11.53	2./ 13	6./ 23	7./ 16	7./ 41	10./ 3	
Chesterfield	dep.		1.10	4.2	8.7	11.55	2./ 17	6./ 26	7./ 18	7./ 45	10./ 5	
Sheffield	arr.	1.5		4.23	8.52	12./ 16	2./ 38	6./ 45	7./ 43	8./ 24	10./ 29	12.10

Above: Nottingham Road, 1906. In 1848 a racecourse was opened north of Derby station and so it was only logical that a station would be built there. After opening in 1856, it, like Derby station, was subject to constant improvements. In 1860 a waiting shed was added and other enlargements were done in 1860, 1867 and 1868. A siding and facilities for unloading horses were built by the Midland Railway. *Author's collection*

Below: Nottingham Road, 1947. This view south illustrated nicely not only the facilities, but also the arrangement for trains. The station served only the passenger lines, with the goods lines passing to the east, seen here with an 0-6-0 on a northbound coal train. The signal gantry shows up nicely, being controlled by Derby North box, just visible beneath the left hand signals on the gantry. The group of four posts on the right are for the passenger lines. These allow movement east to Chaddesden, or onto the slow lines or, as the tallest post indicates, along the up passenger line to Derby station. The slow lines had a choice of east, or to the station. *Stations UK*

Above: St. Mary's goods junction, 1951. The northbound 'Devonian' is captured around 4.15pm on 18 July. Class Five 4-6-0 No.44747 has 4-4-0 No.41088 as pilot. This is a picture full of action. To the left are the goods lines with a train on the down line. To the right are the tracks, complete with two shunting engines, to the goods yard. This area developed as a direct result of congestion at Derby yard. The directors had second thoughts about this yard as they believed some customers might think it was too far for the delivery of materials. However, using the 1848 Parliamentary approval for the Ripley branch, it was built at a cost of £10,000 in 1852. Like most railway infrastructure, it was added to and enlarged over the years, ending up as a double tracked branch with its own controlling signal box. Operationally, it was on the 'wrong' side of the line being adjacent to the passenger lines. The quadruple line arrangement north from here was for the slow lines to flank the central pair of passenger lines.

R J Buckley, Initial Photographics

Below: St Mary's goods yard, 1957. An early July morning train from Manchester to St. Pancras is slowing down ready to stop in Derby station. Compound 4-4-0 No.41150 and its train has just passed under the ex-GNR bridge carrying the line from Nottingham to Derby Friargate. The engine had just three months of its 32 year lifespan left. The last ever appearance of a Compound in regular service was on the North Midland, when Millhouse's No.40907 worked the 9.5am Sheffield-Derby slow on 21 August 1960.

R J Buckley, Initial Photographics

Above: Breadsall Crossing, 1928. MR compound 4-4-0 No.1057, passes the fine signal gantry with a down express. The loco's tender has a modification with coal rails so that it could hold 9 tons of coal, two tons more than the original Deeley design. This was done to help in the non-stop runs to Glasgow and Edinburgh in 1928. In fact, the much publicised non-stop run by the LNER's Flying Scotsman in May 1928 was upstaged by the LMS running the 'Royal Scot' in two parts a few days before. The signals, with the fine splitting distants, are not only for the level crossing, but also for Little Eaton Junction, just over 600 yards north. There the line to Ripley and Butterley branches off east, which, together with loops, was controlled by a 52 lever box on the up side. *V Forster collection*

Below: Breadsall Crossing, 7 September 1940. About to cross Ford Lane are grimy Midland 0-6-0s Nos.4211 & 4405, pulling a heavy coal train north. *H C Casserley*

South of Duffield, 5 July 1958. With the time almost 12.15pm, a Cardiff train which left Newcastle four hours earlier is captured in this picture. It would be almost another six hours before arrival in Cardiff. Hauling this popular, and lengthy, train, is 'Jubilee' class 4-6-0 No.45610 Ghana piloted by ex-MR 4-4-0 No.40540. These two engines would have worked through to Gloucester, where No. 40540 was shedded. Note the method of painting in black/white sections on the post of Peckwash Mill's up slow distant signal, on the right, to make it stand out more. *R J Buckley, Initial Photographics*

South of Duffield, 1959. Looking north sees the 3.7pm special train from Buxton to Derby on 6 September hauled by 2-6-4T No.42184. The signals in the background are for Duffield Junction.
R J Buckley, Initial Photographics

Left, above: Duffield, 1948. The first station with that name dates from 6 April 1841, 11 months after the line north had opened, closing on 1 October 1867, replaced by a station a little further south and opened along with the Wirksworth branch. This view north along the down goods line nicely shows a train using the up slow line to the east of the station. The up passenger platforms were on the right, with road access and the station buildings on the left. Passengers walked to the platforms across the massive wooden footbridge, unfortunately obscuring the signal gantry. The second, longer, bridge was to allow a footpath to cross the line rather than have a level crossing. There was no platform for the up slow line.

Stations UK

Left, below: Duffield, 7 June 1947. Year old Ivatt 2-6-2T No.1206 steams into the branch platform with a service from Wirksworth to Derby, just a few days before the last regular passenger trains ran on 16 June. The branch was retained for freight trains to the quarries at Wirksworth. This view was taken from the footbridge, looking north. The prime reason for the branch's existence was to do with the railway politics of the 1860/70s and the desire of the Midland Railway to tap into the potential of the north-west along its own lines, rather than having to share them with others. This branch could have been extended to Rowsley to connect up with the line to Buxton and Manchester.

R J Buckley, Initial Photographics

Below: Duffield, 1953. To service the branch a single platform was built with a small waiting room. The footbridge, from which this view was taken, connected this platform to the town. Controlling the station and the crossing of trains from the up goods to the branch was this standard Midland box with 38 levers. On 27 June enthusiasts arrived on this special 'High Peaks Rail Tour' pulled by 0-4-4T No.58077. *Stations UK*

Above: North of Duffield, 1952. Passing along the down slow, just passing the site of the first station, and the goods yard at Duffield, is 4F 0-6-0 No.44088 on 7 June. *E R Morten*

Below: Milford Tunnel, 1952. Class 5 4-6-0 No.44986 has just come out of the tunnel and passed the up signals, the arms are backed by white boards to make them stand out. The signal box here also controlled the junction of the goods and passenger lines as only two tracks pass through the tunnel. Note the up gantry and under-slung signals by the signal box. North of the tunnel was an up bracket post with splitting distants for the fast/slow divergence, south of it. Typical English countryside makes up the background. *E R Morten*

Milford Tunnel, 1957. The southern end of the 850 yards long tunnel. Oddly enough, in keeping with other tunnels on the line, the southern portals are 'ordinary' whereas the northern ones are decorative: here they are curved concentric circles. With the time about five past two on 15 June, Class 4 Stanier 2-6-4T No.42431 is heading south. The train will have left Darley Dale thirty-five minutes earlier and will stop at all the stations, except Nottingham Road, to Derby.

B W L Brooksbank, Initial Photographics

Left, above: Belper, circa 1905. The original station buildings were of stone with 'a pronounced Italianate flavour with simple rounded windows and a parapet roof'. They were demolished in 1878 when the station moved just over a kilometre north, the site becoming the goods station. This Edwardian view shows a 2-4-0 with its train of short coaches waiting to travel north at the 'new' station. *Author's collection*

Left, below: Belper, 1903. More than a fair share of the estimated £3,100,000 cost of building the North Midland line is evident in this view north. In all, 12 bridges had to be built in the space of a mile around Belper. The down signal, just visible by the bridge at the end of the platform with a white board behind it for sighting purposes, was moved south to between the fifth and sixth bridge. The platforms were accessed from ramps. Most stations have more facilities on one platform than the other reflecting passenger patronage. Not so here, the up and down platforms have similar, substantial buildings. *Author's collection*

Above: Belper, 1958. With its coupling rods whirring away, the unique diesel-mechanical locomotive No.10100, enters the station with an up train for Derby. Odd as the loco may seem to us now, it needs to be realised that the 1950s were times of great experiments by companies trialling their locos on BR metals. Built at Derby in association with Fell Developments, 10100 had four 500hp Davey Paxman engines. Originally the coupling rod on each side was connected to the four driving wheels. However, minor differences between the two engine's performances meant that a split rod was less likely to suffer damage. Its sheer mass, 116 tons, and shape made it a formidable locomotive. A lot was learnt from the experiment: future diesel locomotives had a large single power unit. A premature end for this loco came on 15 October 1958 when it caught fire in Manchester Central, and it was cut up in Derby in 1960. *Midland Railway Trust*

Belper, 1958. Putting up a fair amount of smoke while passing south is BR Standard class 2-10-0 No.92049, in October. North of the station, the penalty for following river valleys is in evidence. The River Derwent is crossed at Belper Pool by two bridges, Nos.37 & 36. The line crosses the river twice more as well as passing through the short, 101 yards, Longland Tunnel before Ambergate station is reached. The tunnel was opened out into a 65' cutting, and the tracks quadrupled for the mile and a half from Broadholme to Ambergate South Junction, opening towards the end of 1931.

Midland Railway Trust

Above: **Amber Gate, 1840**. The first station had a fine building in a Jacobean style, with mullioned windows, steep pitched roof and Dutch gables. It was sited on the northbound platform north of the 129 yards-long Toadmoor Tunnel. It is interesting to reflect on comments made in 1842 on the '...growing evil of...the railway literally ornamented with so many fine villas....instead of cottage buildings... which would have been sufficient...'

During the Railway Mania of the 1840s, the village was the focal point of the grand sounding Ambergate, Nottingham & Boston & Eastern Junction Railway. It never lived up to the name, only the 19 miles between Colwick and Grantham were ever built.

In 1849 a branch to Rowsley from Ambergate opened, following the Derwent Valley, speculatively built by the Manchester, Buxton, Matlock & Midland Junction Railway – and not serving any of the towns in its name! At that time the branch only had a connection in the northerly direction. In 1852 the line was jointly leased by the Midland and LNWR (the former taking full control in 1871). When the south-to-west curve giving direct access from Derby to Rowsley opened, a second station came into use, in October 1863, situated in the 'V' of the new Ambergate South Junction. The original station building was dismantled in 1864 and re-erected, greatly enlarged, on the new site.

As the Rowsley line extended, the MR was able to access New Mills South Junction in February 1867 and join the Manchester, Sheffield & Lincolnshire Railway, for the final section to Manchester, via Woodley and Guide Bridge. Five London trains traversed the route taking five hours. In 1875 a more direct line via Belle Vue opened and Liverpool coaches were included on the expresses.

Also the Ambergate to Pye Bridge line opened, and Ambergate middle curve was built, so a third station, the familiar triangular one, was constructed, commencing operation in December 1876. The middle curve enabled Derby-Sheffield stopping trains to use the new station; the 1863 station then closed, but found a role as a plans store until the 1960s.

Below: **Ambergate, 1948**. This shows the first station building, as rebuilt and enlarged, adjacent to the main line south of Toadmoor Tunnel, close to Ambergate South Junction. The view is north showing an up passenger train on the main line leaving the tunnel on its way to Derby, having bypassed the famous triangular station, which, in this picture, is served by the line to the left. *Stations UK*

Above: **Ambergate Station Junction, 1948**. On the left in this view is the route to Manchester, with platforms 1 and 2, while on the right are the Clay Cross/Derby lines with platforms 3 and 4. The footbridge, built in 1884, was the only one at the station – it was illuminated too! *Stations UK*

Below: **Ambergate, 1948.** When a six and a half mile line opened from Crich Junction, just north of Ambergate, to Codnor Park Junction on the Erewash Valley line, it allowed coal traffic from the Derbyshire/Nottinghamshire coalfield to get to Manchester and Liverpool without having to pass through Derby. The coal train on the right is on the Manchester line, while curving to the left are the Derby lines. The tall middle signal post is for the down main line, the lower distant is for the easterly branch at Crich Junction. Adjacent, but on the down side, was a set of sorting sidings: entry to these would be indicated by the small arm on the gantry. *Stations UK*

Ambergate West Junction, 1952. Sailing round the curve, after having just started an all stations train from Derby towards Chinley and Manchester is Class Five 4-6-0 No.44838 on 24 May. I suspect there wasn't a queue of staff to fill the oil lamp at the top of the tall signal post on a wet windy day in the winter! Being held at the signals at platform 5 on its way from the Chesterfield direction with a train load of coal is Stanier 8F 2-8-0 No.48379. The wooden platforms and their overhanging nature shows up well.
C H A Townley

61096

THE PALATINE
70017

Left, above: Ambergate, 1960. Cautiously passing platform 2 with a train off the Rowsley line is LNER class B1 4-6-0 No.61096, acting as a reminder that one of the LNER's predecessors, the Great Northern Railway, ran trains from London's Kings Cross through to Manchester via Pinxton, Butterley and Ambergate North! This led to the odd sight of London to Manchester trains actually travelling south at Ambergate North Junction.

Midland Railway Trust

Left, below: Ambergate, I960. A crack express from Manchester to London, 'The Palatine', is creeping through the tight curves – note the check rails. This train, the 2.25pm Manchester Central to St. Pancras, was named by the LMS just before the war, and continued afterwards. The journey time of 3 hours 45 minutes was considered good in those days. A small group of 'Britannia' 4-6-2s was rostered to do some of this work from 1957. The northbound working was the 7.55am from St Pancras. Before the war the timings were 10am ex Manchester and 4.30pm from St Pancras. There was also the 'Peaks Express' in those days, 10.30am down and 4.25pm up. The route was having its Indian Summer in 1960, as modernisation from Euston to Crewe and Manchester London Road (later to emerge as Piccadilly) meant that through services were temporarily switched to the ex-Midland main line. When the rebuilding was finished, services reverted to the ex-L&NWR route. Currently services from Derby only go as far as Matlock, from where Peak Rail runs the preserved line to Rowsley.

Midland Railway Trust

Above: Ambergate, 2 August 1941. Waiting at platform 3 is the 9.28am departure for Mansfield. It will travel north a short distance to Crich Junction, then east via Butterley and will briefly traverse the Erewash Valley line at Pye Bridge before branching off towards Kirkby-in-Ashfield. The loco, 4-4-2T No.2121, is a London, Tilbury & Southend Railway type, but actually built by the LMS in 1925. Platform 3 was also used by trains between Derby and Chesterfield. *H C Casserley*

Above: Ambergate, 1957. Approaching is a loaded coal train on its way to Rowsley hauled by No. 44202. Ahead of it is the West Junction and the line from Derby. Meanwhile, waiting at the Manchester to Clay Cross platform is a load of empties with another 0-6-0, No.43650 at the helm. Ahead of it is the North Junction and the line from Derby. *Midland Railway Trust*

Right, above: Ambergate North Junction, circa 1960. Really this was two junctions very close together. Class 5 4-6-0 No.44945 is heading south and has just passed over one of the junctions. The line it is on goes through Toadmoor Tunnel to the South Junction, avoiding Ambergate station. The lines diverging to the left will split again, just behind the photographer, into a westerly pair for the Manchester platforms and West Junction, and a southern pair for the Derby/Clay Cross platforms at the station. The Manchester and Derby lines meet again at Station Junction, the third side of the Ambergate triangle, and, after a short distance, join the South Junction. *Midland Railway Trust*

Right, below: Ambergate, 1959. Preserved Midland compound No.1000 made its first run in preservation on a special trip from Birmingham to York on 31 August. Here it is taking the Ambergate avoiding line, with Crich Junction ahead as it passes the North Junction's up signals. The ones on the left are for Ambergate station's Derby platform, with the Manchester line's signals on the shorter post. Also on the gantry, just out of shot, are the main (avoiding) line signals and others controlling the up reception line, from which the photograph was taken. *Frank Ashley*

1000
1000

44802

WINGFIELD

Left, above: South of Wingfield, 8 May 1954. Many people's impression of the Midland Railway is of small engines, with trains being double headed. While this was undoubtedly true, double heading was still needed even when larger, more powerful, engines came on the scene due to longer and heavier trains being the order of the day. Here, two Class 5 4-6-0s are needed if the Newcastle to Bristol train is to keep to its timings. No.44802 pilots a Caprotti variation of the same class. *E R Morten*

Left, below: Wingfield, 1951. North of Ambergate, the line follows the course of the River Amber, crossing it twice, the Cromford Canal crosses the line by Bull Bridge, and the short (260 yards) Lodge Hill (or Wingfield) tunnel is traversed, all in the three miles to Wingfield station. The station here was 'for Alfreton, Mansfield etc...'. This view south shows the staggered platforms well. It is interesting to note that while prominent notices usually deter passengers from crossing the line, here it was the accepted mode of transfer between platforms. The station was built by Radford of Alfreton and has been described as 'the finest of all station houses. Its well proportioned booking hall and flanking bays, attractive low pitched roofs with projecting eaves and simple windows create an overall perfection'. A sculptured clock surround was above the doorway and, for its day, the chimney stacks were fanciful. However, such architectural gems were not without critics, especially on the entrance to the gentleman's lavatory: 'So exposed... as naturally to shock the female travellers who cannot fail to observe the constant bustle about these buildings, and more especially when the bell rings for the departure of the train'. An entrance lobby was recommended. Corridors and lavatories in train carriages were not available when this was written! *Stations UK*

Above: Wingfield, 29 July 1960. This view was taken from the end of the up platform, looking north. About to race through is the 12.30pm from York, headed by 'Jubilee' class 4-6-0 No. 45576 *Bombay*. The permanent way gang – in the days before reflective safety clothing – stand clear. The down platform hosts a small shelter. North of the station was the branch to Shirland Colliery. *R J Buckley, Initial Photographics*

Above: Stretton, 1948. The station was called Smithy Moor for the first few months after opening in April 1841, changing to Stretton during the year. Thirty years later, on 1 October 1872, it became Stretton for Ashover until closure almost ninety years later on 11 September 1961. In this view looking north, taken from the overbridge, is a typical MR signal box and the trailing slip to the goods yard on the down side. The reason why there are both home and distant signals on the signal post is that just under the bridge are the up and down goods loops. At 360' above sea level, Stretton was the highest point on the North Midland line. The south end of Clay Cross Tunnel is just around the bend. After an 18 mile climb from Derby, the line now falls in the Rother valley all the way to Wath, some 29 miles north. Stretton was the scene of an interesting accident in 1844. A northbound coal train was about to back into the down siding so that a faster moving passenger train to the rear could overtake it. However, the driver stopped the train just short of the points, and so had to restart the train. As he did so, a coupling towards the rear of the train broke. As repairs were being done, a down double headed passenger train ran into the rear of the coal train, with lots of damage, but no casualities. The guard had been sent back along the line to warn the oncoming train of the obstruction, but he didn't, and so was fined £2 with 13/- costs. *Stations UK*

Below: Near to the main line was the basic halt at Stretton which served the short-lived passenger service on the narrow gauge Ashover Light Railway. *RAS Marketing*

Ashover Light Railway

Although the Ashover Light Railway did not open until 1925, the concept of tapping into the resources of the area had been in place since the North Midland Railway was being built in the late 1830s. The building of the Clay Cross Tunnel allowed the deeper than surface exploration of the geology of the area. The tunnel was '...driven through wet coal measures...', the bricks for the tunnel were made in a local factory and iron ore was discovered. So profitable, and demanding so much time, were these enterprises that in 1837 George Stephenson moved from Alton Grange in Leicestershire to rent Tapton House near Chesterfield, overlooking the forming North Midland Railway. He, and a group of others, bought a large piece of land near to the proposed southern portal of the tunnel. A trading company. 'George Stephenson & Co.' with his Secretary Charles Binns as General Manager was established. It needs to be remembered that at that time engines ran not on coal, but on coke. The company saw the NMR as not only a means of transporting coal, but also as a user for the coke that could be made from it. This enterprise was so profitable that when the line opened in 1840, the collieries were able to not only supply all the NMR locos but they were able also to send train loads to London from 1845: this trade increasing to one-third of a million tons per year later. The village of Clay Cross rapidly expanded by a factor of almost three from 1831 to 1841. Many workers came for the construction of the tunnel and stayed. After his death in 1848 – all the shops in Chesterfield closed for the day of his funeral – Stephenson's son, Robert, took a greater part in the running of the company. In 1852 he left the company, which changed its name to the 'Clay Cross Company'. It was a very paternalistic firm providing money and land for the building of homes, churches, Mechanics Institute and free education for employees' children from 1854. Over the next 30 years more collieries, a third blast furnace and a foundry for making cast iron pipes were built. A gas plant was developed, supplying not only the works, but also the surrounding 40 square miles.

That the Ashover area, to the west of Clay Cross, was rich in minerals was never in doubt. In fact in 'Mining Journal Vol. 3' in 1839 it was reported that a line from Ashover to join the NMR near Clay Cross had been surveyed and agreement with landowners entered into, but these plans came to nothing. An extract from the Overton Estate sales catalogue in 1869 stated that 'the quantity of limestone and gritstone upon this (Ashover) estate is almost inexhaustible' from which a large income could be derived.

Another scheme for the MR to build a three and a half mile branch from Stretton to Alton Colliery was proposed: two years later the mine closed. It was not until after the Great War, in 1919, that the Overton Estate was purchased by the Clay Cross Company, reviving interest in a rail connection. The purpose of the line was to transport 500 tons a day of limestone and 100 tons a day of fluorspar and other minerals. Alton Colliery could produce 400 tons a day and the line would be able to carry milk to the main line station as well as passengers as this was an area much sought after by tourists. The line was to be standard gauge from Stretton, passing south-west to Ashover. In an attempt to reduce costs as much as possible as the line crossed several public roads and was not all on land they owned, and so would involve compulsory purchase of land, the company wanted to avoid the expense of two public investigations. So they utilised the Light Railways Acts of 1896/1912. This meant lower standards of signalling, lower speeds and axle loadings. The line was to pass south from a point adjacent to the MR station at Stretton, and at the end of the down loop a connection between the two was to be provided. At the narrow gauge station a stairway to the MR lines was to be provided to allow passenger transfers. Stretton had 26,000 passengers a year and the exchange facility was a feature of the ALR passenger services, being timed to allow connections at Stretton. As the 1920s was a time of depression, the Clay Cross Company directors decided to extend the line north to their works and to reduce it to 60cm gauge: for the same money as a standard gauge line they could have a longer line. Savings of 2/- per ton compared to carting coal to Ambergate were quoted, excluding income from other minerals. At the 1922 public inquiry it was stated that residents of the Amber Valley had complained at the prospect of building lime kilns at Ashover and so the Company's plans to transport the stone to Clay Cross was welcome – a passenger service was also proposed. In 1922 the War Disposal Board was selling off large quantities of 60 cm stock, much of it unused, that had been supplied for the Great War. Lt. Colonel Stephens was retained to build the line for the company, buying four Baldwin 4-6-0 tank engines, subsequently named after one of the directors' children. The line opened for passengers just in time for Easter 1925, 7 April.

However, the East Midlands Motor Services Ltd. offered an improved service in both frequency and comfort compared to a few years previously. Both organisations charged the same fare, 1/3d, but the trains were slower and a change needed to be made at Stretton. As regards convenience, there was no comparison. So drastic was the decline in passengers that in 1931 the service was cut to Wednesdays and weekends only. By 1935/6 it was reduced again to Summer time only, and then most passengers were carried on Bank Holidays. Ordinary services consisted of one coach, usually empty, at the head of a train of goods wagons. On 13 September 1936 the passenger service was 'suspended until further notice.' The line reverted to its primary purpose, goods, which was buoyant. Operating losses mounted in spite of increasing amount of goods carried, so much so that due to the investment needed it was decided to close the line from 31 March 1950.

Clay Cross Tunnel. The rock outcrop that the 1784 yards-long Clay Cross Tunnel penetrates is a watershed. To the south are the valleys of the rivers Amber and Derwent, while north is the Rother. This area is also the highest point on the line from Derby to Leeds, with gradients no greater than 1 in 330 leading to it. While this was an undoubted strength when talking to prospective backers, and in early operations, it soon became a liability. Following river valleys is fine, as long as they go past the towns the line needs to serve. While a tunnel had to be built here, the subsequent route north took the valley, shallow gradient, route and avoided main centres of population like Sheffield, Barnsley and Wakefield.

Although the estimated cost of the tunnel was £98,000 the actual cost was £140,000 when dug. As this would take the longest to build along the line, it was the first contract let, work commencing on 2 February 1837. Six shafts were dropped allowing 12 working faces, this extending to 22 as reported to the NMR Board in April 1839. Originally, there was to be a station in the middle due to its proximity to the town. However, the width of the shaft and the difficulty of clearing the tunnel of smoke led to this idea being shelved. Local coal deposits and uses for the limestone (for lime making and iron ore smelting later) were spin-offs for the area from this project. As previously mentioned, George Stephenson formed a company exploiting local ore initially, and later from further afield.

The navvies who built railway lines had many run-ins with local populations. Here was no exception, being accused of sheep rustling as well as the usual drunkenness and petty theft. It needs to be remembered that wages were often on the token system. These were exchanged for goods only at the railway company's shop where the workers were 'ripped off', it took an Act of Parliament to stop this practise. The tunnel was completed by August 1839, with a human cost of fifteen workers losing their lives during construction. The portals had ornamental stone work, the northern one here resembling a magnificent Moorish gateway, it is now listed as a Grade II building. One of the ventilation shafts has seats around it in Market Street, Clay Cross, while the one on High Street is nearly 150' above the line, which is at its highest point, 500' above sea level.

Robert Gratton

Above: Clay Cross and Egstow. The terminus of the Ashover Light Railway shown here was almost above the main line tunnel. One of the Baldwin 4-6-0 tanks stands at the modest station. *Topical Press Agency*

Below: Clay Cross South Junction, 1964. Clanking along is a WD 'Austerity' 2-8-0 with a northbound train of coal empties. Having come from the Derby direction it is on the down main line that has just been joined by the passenger lines from Trent. On the right are the lines to the Town Goods, while the pair of lines on the left are the goods lines. It is onto this pair of lines that the train will be switched, north of the station. The controlling signal box is just above the wagons on the left. *G Perrin*

Above: Clay Cross station, 1841. This consisted of a small rectangular building and staggered platforms. Adjacent was a water tank and a pumping house, built to match.

Below: Clay Cross station, 1900s. In May 1879 the Erewash Valley line from Trent joined the ex-NMR line just north of the tunnel. This view north shows the two platforms built when the station became a junction, with covered steps down from the wooden booking office on the adjacent overbridge. These became the fast lines and another pair of lines was built to the east which became the slow lines. All four lines carried on down the Erewash Valley to Trent, Nottingham and further south towards London. Of interest is the MR practice of putting a black spot on the back of its stop signals. *Author's collection*

Above: Clay Cross, 1931. Passing along the up slow line with loaded coal wagons is Wellingborough based Beyer-Garratt 2-6-0+0-6-2 No.4991 on 4 April. Although one would have expected these engines to be equivalent to two 2-6-0s ('Crabs') this is not how they were regarded by the operating department of the LMS. They were rated as being equal to the power of two 0-6-0s, one 4F and one 3F. Of course there were great savings in train crews, the downside was that they were operationally limited due to their length and weight as well as being restricted to facilities that could handle the very long trains – between 90 to 100 wagons – that they hauled. This engine still has the rectangular coal bunker above the water tank on the rear power unit, and could carry seven tons of coal. Some had rails fitted to increase the capacity and an experiment was tried with a steam operated coal pusher on No.4996. By 1932, a rotating coal bunker, with nine tons capacity, later increased to ten, was fitted. *Author's collection*

Below: Clay Cross, 1932. Signalled to pass onto the Erewash Valley line is Garratt No.4988 on 14 May. The load of coal is probably bound for Toton yard. The Garratts were renumbered in the 7967-7999 series from 1938 to make way for the increasing numbers of Stanier Class 5s being constructed at the time. *E R Morten*

Above: Clay Cross, 30 August 1925. By 1895, the MR had concentrated its goods facilities for the town on a mile long goods branch. This was accessed from just south of the station with sidings adjacent to it. The line passed up over the Derby line before the northern tunnel entrance, and from Coney Green sidings on the Erewash Valley line, to meet in the goods depot. Shunting in the sidings by the station is MR 0-4-0ST No.1522. This wheel arrangement is not normally associated with the MR, 0-6-0 being the usual configuration. The class this engine belongs to owes its design to Johnson who needed some short wheelbase engines for shunting in areas with tight curvature. Prior to renumbering and repainting around 1910, it would have been in crimson livery with brass numberplates. No. 1522 was built at Derby in 1897 and entered service with the duplicate No.1138A. The saddle tanks could hold 650 gallons of water, while the fireman is scooping up some of the 8cwt that the side bunker could hold.

LCGB, Ken Nunn collection

Below: Clay Cross engine shed, August 1954. In the shed is ex-MR 0-6-0T No.41763. This single road affair, complete with doors, was still in operation long after the structure appeared to be unsafe – the leaning chimney of Clay Cross is an unknown wonder of the world!

RAS Marketing

Above: Clay Cross, 1950s. The island platform, flanked by two single faced ones, shows up well in this view north. Racing through on the up fast line is a 'Black 5' 4-6-0 with at least nine coaches. On the far platform can be seen the signals controlling the crossovers from the slow lines at the north end of the station. For the passenger lines there was a four arm bracket signal partially obscured by the smoke. Both sets of signals were operated from the 56 lever Clay Cross North Junction box, alas hidden in the smoke too. *Stations UK*

Below: Clay Cross, North Junction, 1963. The long up freight train hauled by Stanier 8F 2-8-0 No.48421 is bound for Derby. It has just crossed over from the up goods line, across the down goods, to access this route. Careful diagramming of such trains was very important, not only as they blocked lines in making the above manoeuvre, but also because the next available passing place was south of the tunnel at Stretton. Realistically, with trains of this length, the next piece of quadruple track was south of Milford tunnel, some nine miles ahead. Thus any passenger train would have to wait until this train had cleared the line before passing it. *G Perrin*

Above: Avenue sidings, early 1960s. A typical Midland freight, hauled by an ageing 0-6-0 passes along the up fast line, probably destined for the Derby area. During excavations for the southern extension to Avenue sidings, coal was discovered with 5,000 tons being sold – not unlike the works over 100 years earlier at Clay Cross Tunnel. Part of the River Rother was culverted in the process. The coking plant was west of the lines and as Avenue sidings was to the east, a flyover was built to stop movements between the two from fouling the main running lines – the gradient was 1 in 100 up to the bridge and 1 in 175 down into the site. It was across here that the National Coal Board's diesel engines would shuttle with 30 wagons. The flyover is in the distance in this view, emphasising the length of the sidings. *G Perrin*

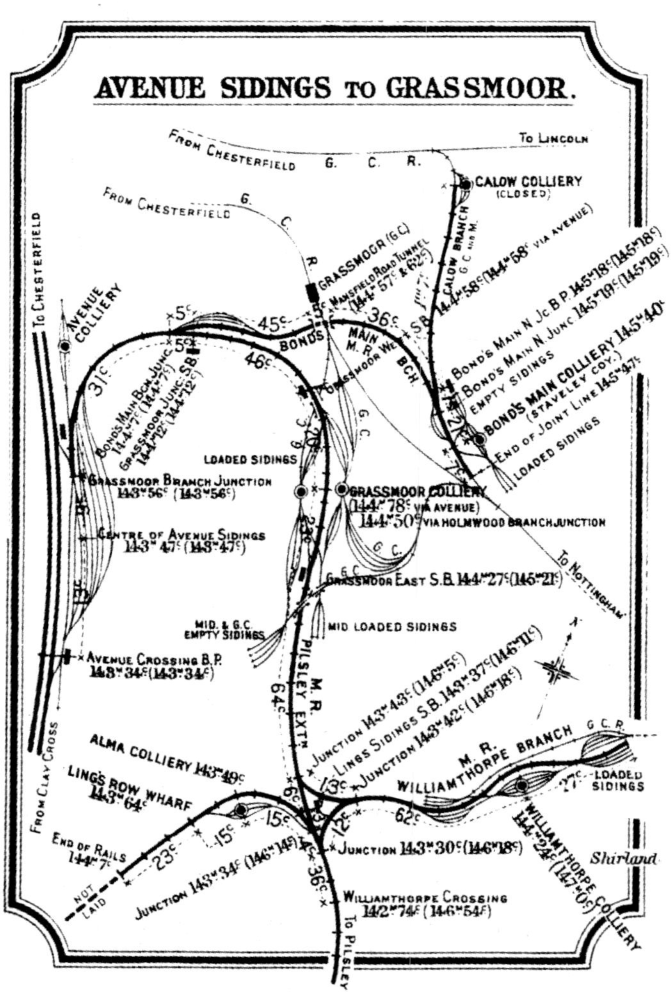

Right, above: Avenue sidings. A large number of pits (e.g. Bond's Main, Grassmoor and Williamthorpe as well as Grassmoor coke ovens) to the east and north-east of Clay Cross were connected by the Grassmoor Branch. These formed a series of 15 loops which were connected to the main line at Avenue Sidings, just over a mile north of Clay Cross. To accommodate the Coking Plant at Avenue, in the early 1950s British Railways planned to lay out some loops attached to the southern end of Avenue Sidings, on the site of Ryknild Street, a Roman road. They actually built six very long loops, each capable of holding two complete trains. An unidentified 8F is arriving with a load of coal wagons. One could arrive from the north, reverse in and at the same time one from the south could be similarly dealt with. In this way the engines were able to be released easily. At the southern end they joined three loops exiting by Clay Cross North box. *G Perrin*

Right, below: Avenue sidings, 1960s. Shunting at the southern end of the loops is Stanier 8F 2-8-0 No.48200. The loaded coal wagons were marshalled into smaller groups ready to be taken into the coking plant by their own engines, one can be seen in the middle of the picture. It is odd that large quantities of coal were transported about in relatively small wagons. Part of the problem was that, especially when the collieries were privately owned, they had different, and restricted, screens for loading wagons. They were reluctant to spend money on altering a system that would give them no benefits but would make the railways more efficient. The standardisation for Merry-Go-Round trains from the early 1970s was a major feat for the railways. *B Tebb*

Above: Hasland sidings signal box. This typical MR wooden box is seen from the window of a down passenger train. Its 55 levers chiefly controlled access to the adjacent engine shed. The box closed in 1969. Behind are the sidings associated with the Avenue plant. *G Perrin*

Below: Hasland, 1960. Scurrying along the up fast on a fitted freight is Standard Class 2-10-0 No.92155. In contrast to the Beyer-Garratts these well-designed locomotives were very versatile, being used on all types of main line passenger and freight work. *Midland Railway Trust*

Hasland sidings, 1955. One of the named train to pass this way was the 'Devonian'. Bristol Barrow Road shed's 'Jubilee' class No.45699 *Galatea* is in charge, passing an 'Austerity' and an 8F on the slow lines. This express went from Bradford Forster Square to Bristol and then on the ex-GWR route to Torquay and Kingswear, a 10 hour journey.
Midland Railway Trust

List of places and customers served at Clay Cross and Hasland as shown in Railway Clearing House 'Official Handbook of Railway Stations' 1938 edition

Clay Cross

Station, sidings	Position
Clay Cross Co:	
Brickwork Siding	Clay Cross
Iron Works	Clay Cross
Coney Green Siding	Clay Cross and Chesterfield
Danesmoor (Clay Cross Colliery No. 7)	Clay Cross and Doe Hill
Doncaster Wagon Co Siding	Clay Cross
Hepthorne Lane Sidings	Clay Cross
Town	Clay Cross

Hasland

Station, sidings	Position
Avenue Sidings	Hasland
Chesterfield RDC	Hardwick Collieries
Clay Cross Co. Bond's Main Colliery	Bond' s Main branch
Grassmoor Colliery	Grassmoor branch
Hardwick By-Products Co, siding	Grassmoor branch
Hardwick Collieries	Grassmoor branch
Ling's Row Wharf	Grassmoor branch
Staveley Coal & Iron, Bond's Main Brickworks	Clay Cross Co Bond's Main Colliery
Williamthorpe Colliery	Grassmoor branch

Hasland shed, 2 March 1958. Standing out in the shed yard is Garratt No.47994. Except for special lines at Toton, elsewhere these long engines were stabled outside. The allocation of Garratts to Hasland was for traffic along the Hope Valley line to Gowhole, although, occasionally, they would work the York & North Midland line, from Normanton to York. This engine was the last survivor of the class. Having run her last revenue earning trip from Toton two days earlier, she languished here until departure for cutting up at Crewe on 14 March. *N Stead*

Hasland shed, 1954. This exposed view shows the construction well, as viewed from across the turntable. This is the middle section of the shed – between the end walls were lattice girders that the roof members rested upon, these girders were supported by double iron uprights. As a Midland shed it was coded No.23. The LMS put it under Toton's wing as 18C. The types of engines represented in this picture shows the Midland in this area as principally a mover of goods, with five of the six engines being of the 0-6-0 wheel arrangement – 58153, 44603, 43959, 44244 and 44151. The sole passenger engine is MR 4-4-0 No.40502. *RAS Marketing*

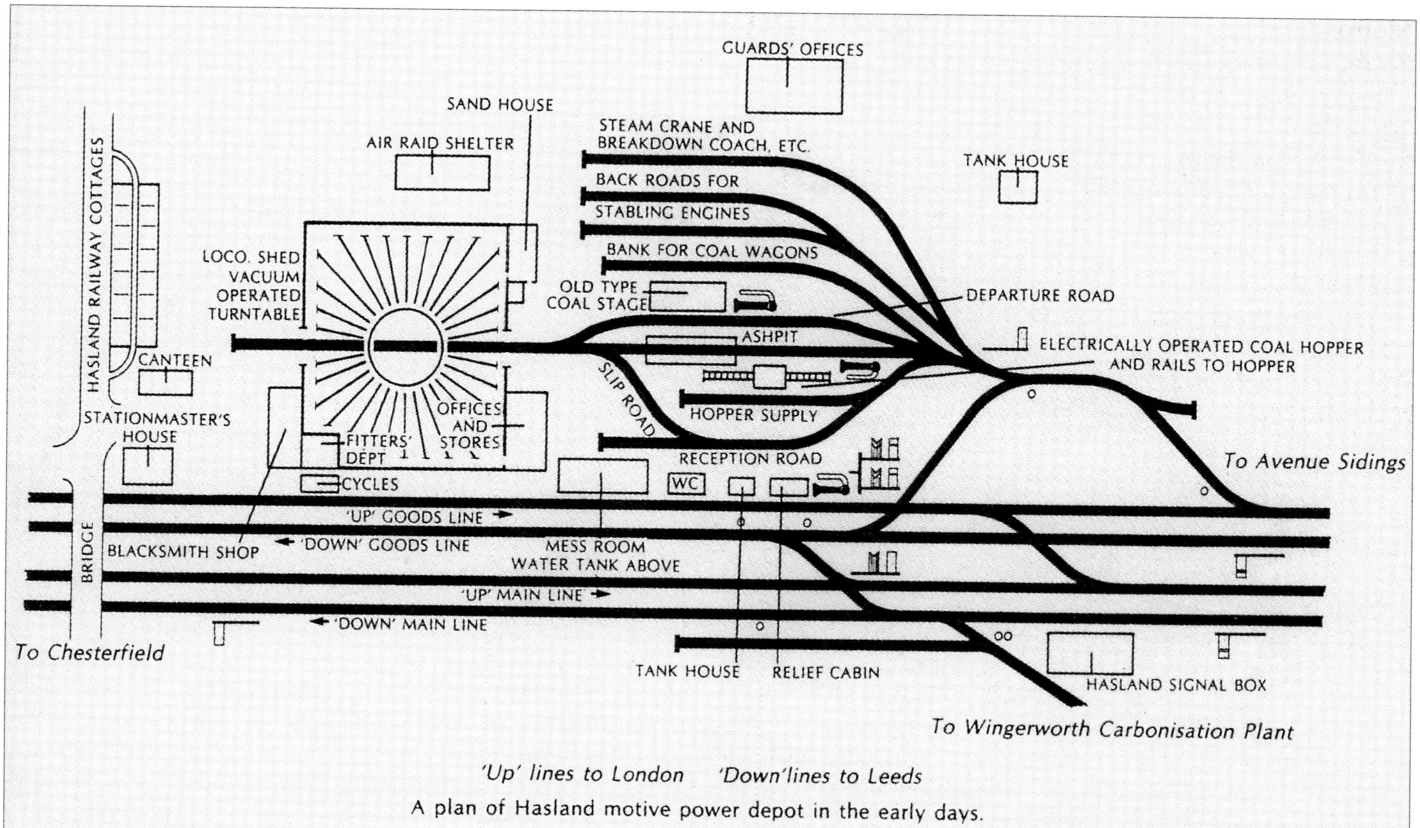

'Up' lines to London 'Down'lines to Leeds

A plan of Hasland motive power depot in the early days.

Above: Leaving Chesterfield, 2 September 1955. On a short mixed southbound goods approaching Hasland is MR 0-6-0 3F No.43650. The town regarded itself as the 'Metropolis of the Derbyshire Coalfield', its celebrated crooked spire can be seen in the background.

H C Casserley

Right: Horns Bridge.

Half a mile before Chesterfield station was a marvellous place for watching trains. In 1893 the Manchester Sheffield & Lincolnshire Railway built the Chesterfield Loop, a stone's throw to the west of the 1840 MR line. It swung east, passing under the older line. Footbridges crossed the line to connect Clayton Street with Lordsmill Street and Hasland Road. The road bridge under the MR line was rebuilt in 1932 to allow single-decker buses to pass under it. After floods in 1931 it was the GC line that was under water. Leaping across the top, in an east to west direction, was the 1897 Lancashire, Derbyshire & East Coast Railway from its Market Place station east to Langwith Junction. With its 700' long viaduct of seven brick arches and four girder sections, 63' above the River Rother, it dominated the skyline until the last arch was demolished in 1984. Pearson's, the builders, took nine months to construct the structure. It may look like a viaduct designed by a committee but the different spans and supports that were necessary required various solutions. From the west it was made up of a 25' arch rising from the embankment followed by a 60' arch over the Derby Road. A 115' bow string girder was next, crossing the quadruple MR main line with the Hasland Road under it. The 40' brick arch that followed had the words 'Dukeries Route' painted on it. Then three lattice plate girders carried the line 50' above the MS&LR, which passed at an angle through the middle span. Finally four 25' brick arches took the line to the high ground to the east, the River Rother passing under the first two.

The grand ideas of the LD&ECR were readily taken on board by the population of the day. It promised to '...revolutionise the district, to revive stagnating industries, to stimulate the whole trade of the locality and make the ancient Borough one of the most important of the many centres of commercial activity in the UK.' The line would connect the East and West coasts of England and open out the wealthy coalfield beneath Chesterfield. There was also the intention to transport day trippers to Sherwood Forest along the line.

The photographer was very patient. On the LD&EC line, there were probably only five passenger trains a day each way, and so he was extremely lucky to have caught an eastbound passenger train for Lincoln with a 'C' class 0-4-4T tank engine in charge, crossing the viaduct at the same time as an MR goods train was passing. The fine signal, complete with lower repeater arms, was replaced by an equally tall bracket signal, with just home arms, some time later.

B Taylor collection

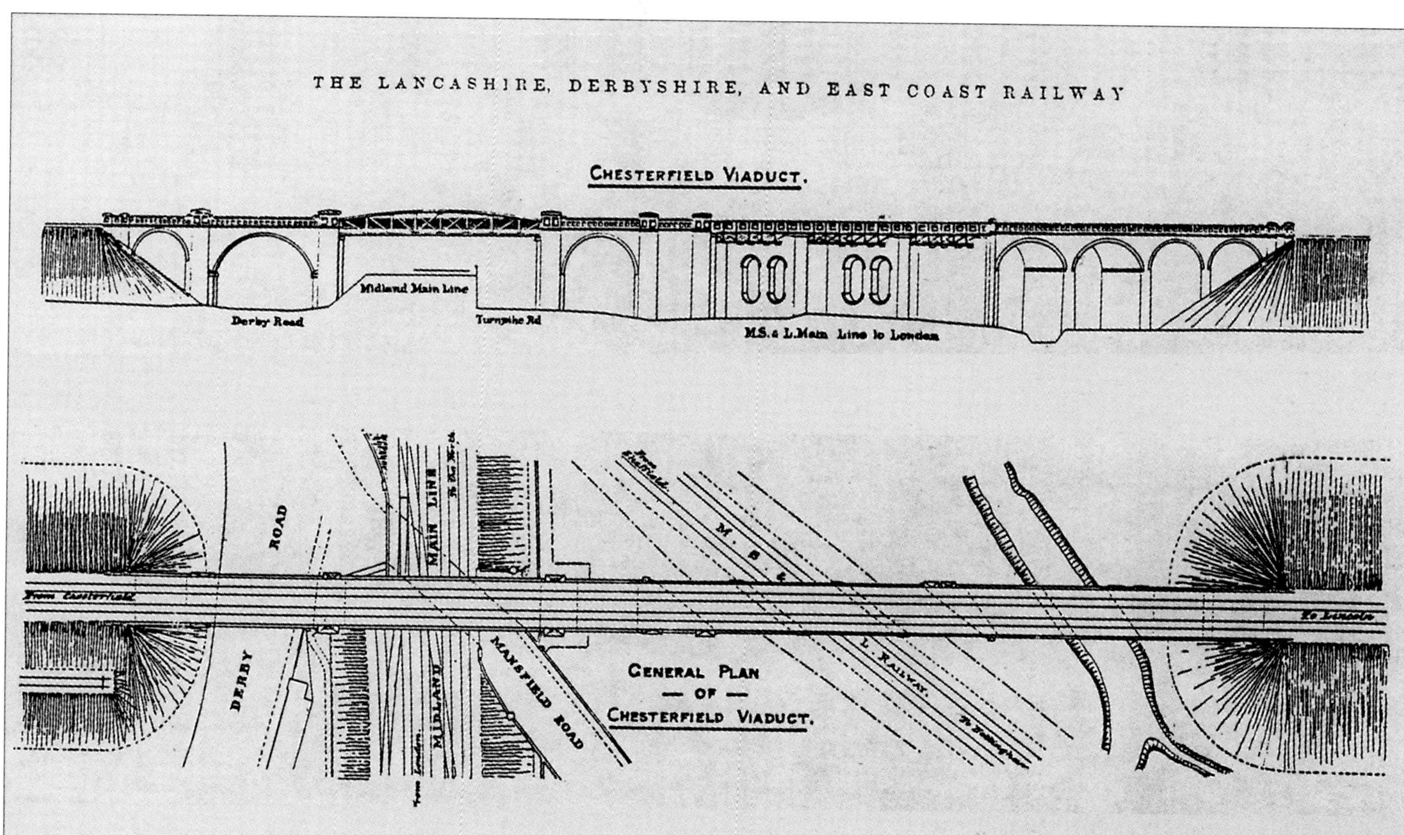
THE LANCASHIRE, DERBYSHIRE, AND EAST COAST RAILWAY
CHESTERFIELD VIADUCT.
Midland Main Line
Derby Road
Turnpike Rd
M.S. & L. Main Line to London
DERBY ROAD
MAIN LINE
MIDLAND
MANSFIELD ROAD
From Sheffield
M. S. & L. RAILWAY.
To Lincoln
GENERAL PLAN
— OF —
CHESTERFIELD VIADUCT.

Brampton branch, pre-grouping. This one and a half mile line south of Chesterfield station opened in 1873, serving a host of industries – chemical, electricity, pottery, stone, engineering, Boythorpe and Brampton collieries as well as the inevitable gas works. Looking east, possibly from the chimney of Wheatbridge Mills, gives a panoramic view not only of the Midland Railway coal and goods sidings there, but also the rival ex-LD&ECR's goods yard. The Brampton branch splits into two here. One line is shown passing over Boythorpe Road at the level crossing. It also crosses the River Hipper twice in this view. The other fork is hidden by the kiln chimneys of Wheatbridge Potteries, branching off to the top left to serve the town's gas works, and Brampton Brewery too. The GC goods yard was very extensive, and judging by the number of wagons, well used. The large two-storey brick building is that company's goods shed and to the right of it is Market Place station, fronting onto West Bars. While the station was more in the centre of the town than the Midland's, it needs to be remembered that it was meant to be a through station on a line from Warrington, between Liverpool & Manchester, to Sutton-on-Sea and so allow outlets to both west and east coasts for coal. The engineering works to push the line westwards would have been very extensive: this is as far west as the line was built.
P Kaye

Brampton Branch, circa 1963. Ex-LMS 0-6-0T No.47535 is waiting to join the down goods feeder track, a ground frame controlled this manouevre. The extensive goods yard, with both the wooden and brick buildings still standing, was accessed from this loop, a 55' turntable also being provided. On the left is Hollis Lane Signal Box which controlled a set of sidings and connections to Broad Oaks Iron Works accessed from the slow lines. The flat building was Markham & Co, set up by Charles Markham, who, with Matthew Kirtley, developed a system in 1859 at Derby that allowed engines to burn coal. Until then, more expensive coke had to be used.

G Perrin

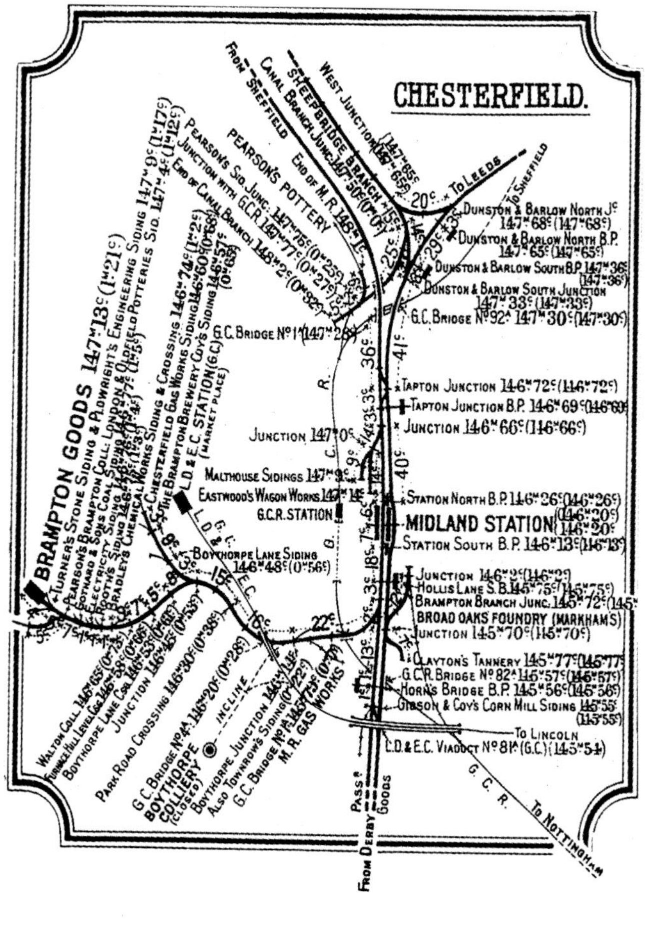

Above: Chesterfield, exterior, 1840.This was probably the largest of the intermediate stations. It was built ...' in the Jacobethan style (like Ambergate) but with plain gables, with a large centre bay... '. Here too a water tank and pumping station were constructed in similar style stone.

Below: Chesterfield, interior, circa 1865. Still basically recognisable even though an extensive canopy was added around 1860. In 1870 the station closed, to be replaced by one 100 yards north. Note the tall signal. The locomotive is one of the famous 'Jenny Lind' class, built at Derby. *Author's collection*

Chesterfield, exterior, circa 1900. The Midland station as it looked at the turn of the century. Not 300 yards to the west was the Great Central station in the town with the Lancashire, Derbyshire & East Coast terminus at Market Place a mile west. Looking at the picture you wouldn't think that there was hot competition for passengers! Following the closure of all licensed premises by order of the Magistrate on 19 August 1911, a riot broke out in the town. A mob besieged the railway staff in the station here breaking many windows. The Mayor read the Riot Act and even charges by the police failed to disperse the mob. The arrival of the West Riding Regiment, with fixed bayonets, did the job. Units of the Gordon Highlanders and the Dublin Fusiliers helped restore peace: 24 arrests were made.

Author's collection

Chesterfield, interior,1912. Edwardian dress, adverts and milk churns make up this pre-Great War view. There were only the two through platforms as shown here, although up and down bays were added later. The goods lines, to the east of the station, were opened in 1874. *Author's collection*

Above: Chesterfield, exterior, 1956. A description of the 1870 station, shown here, states: 'The building will be of the Gothic style, constructed of red pressed brick with white brick pilasters and cornices of Ransome stone on the approach sides. The cornices on the platform sides will be of coloured brick and encaustic tiles, the arches of the windows will be of coloured brick. The building will consist of three parts, the central one being the booking hall two storeys high and open to the roof. The single storey south wing will contain the waiting rooms, and the north wing the station masters' , parcels, telegraph and porters rooms. On the up side will be a waiting room, an underground passage will provide access to the up platform. Both platforms will have ornamental trim roof supported by iron pillars.'

In 1963-65 the station was knocked down and rebuilt, while alterations costing £300,000 were agreed in 1992 to give us today's station. Chesterfield won 'Best Kept Station' awards in 1968 and 1969. *H C Casserley*

Below: Chesterfield, interior, 1958. In 1950 the suffix 'St Mary's' was added to the name, only to be replaced by 'Midland' the next year. This view north not only shows the facilities well but also an engine just poking out from behind the coach in the up bay, as it passes on the up goods line. *Stations UK*

Two pictures from the 1930s.
Above: Chesterfield, 1936. Heading south is ex-MR 4-4-0 No.926. Of interest is the lining of the paint work on the signal box and the home signal on its concrete slotted post. The two bays, one with a platform face, have their own arms. The ends of the platforms here are over the River Rother. *H C Casserley*

Below: Chesterfield, 1933. The station is in the background as this mixture of coaching stock sets off along the down fast line on 5 March, hauled by Hughes-Fowler 'Crab' 2-6-0 No.13123. On the right are the wagon construction and repair workshops belonging to Chesterfield Wagon Works. Waiting on the up slow is a light engine; the signals make a fine background. *E R Morten*

Passenger trains between Chesterfield and Derby from the LMS time table dated October 1st 1934

(Trains travelling a shorter distance, i.e. Chesterfield to Ambergate or Duffield to Derby are not shown)

Weekday service												
Sheffield	dep.	1.15	4.42	6.21	7.58	8.10	9.24	11.47	11.47	1./ 52	2./ 5	3./ 1
Chesterfield	arr.	1.41	5.7	6.53	8.29	8.48	9.43		12./ 16	2./ 16	2./ 43	3./ 33
Chesterfield	dep.	1.44	5.16	6.57	8.33	8.52	9.46		12./ 21	2./ 19	2./ 47	3./ 35
Clay Cross				7.7		9. 0			12./ 29		2./ 55	
Stretton (for Ashover)				7.14		9.7			12./ 37		3./ 3	
Wingfield				7.20		9.12			12./ 43		3./ 10	
Ambergate				7.27		9.22	10.7		12./ 51		3./ 19	3./ 55
Belper			5.43	7.34		9.29			12./ 58		3./ 27	
Duffield			5.50	7.40		9.37			1./ 5		3./ 34	
Derby, Nottingham Road				H								
Derby	arr.	2.22	5.58	7.51	9.3	9.45	10.19	12./ 40	1./ 13	2./ 49	3./ 43	4./ 11
		MX										

Weekday service									
Sheffield	dep.	3./ 56	4./ 50	5./ 12	6./ 21	8./ 0	8./ 49	11./ 18	11./ 45
Chesterfield	arr.	4./ 28	5./ 14	5./ 42	6./ 46	8./ 19	9./ 20	11./ 40	12.7
Chesterfield	dep.	4./ 33	5./ 17	5./ 44	6./ 49	8./ 22	9./ 24	11./ 46	12.10
Clay Cross		4./ 41		5./ 52	6./ 58		9./ 32		
Stretton (for Ashover)		4./ 48		5./ 59	7./ 5		9./ 39		
Wingfield		4./ 54		6./ 6	7./ 11		9./ 45		
Ambergate		5./ 3		6./ 20	7./ 21	8./ 42	9./ 53		
Belper				6./ 27			9./ 59		
Duffield				6./ 35			10./ 7		
Derby, Nottingham Road									
Derby	arr.	5./ 17	5./ 48	6./ 43	7./ 35	8./ 57	10./ 15	12.18	12.44

12.44	a.m. trains
11./ 45	p.m. trains
H	Stops to set down only

Sunday service										
Sheffield	dep.	1.15	4.42	9.9	1./ 21	4./ 10	6./ 12	8./ 5	11./ 13	11./ 45
Chesterfield	arr.	1.41	5.7	9.48	1./ 43	4./ 49	6./ 36	8./ 27	11./ 40	12.7
Chesterfield	dep.	1.44	5.16	9.52	1./ 47	4./ 54	6./ 40	8./ 30	11./ 46	12.10
Clay Cross				10. 0		5./ 3				
Stretton (for Ashover)				10.7		5./ 12				
Wingfield				10.13		5./ 20				
Ambergate			5.36	10.21	2./ 10	5./ 31	7./ 0			
Belper			5.43	10.28		5./ 38				
Duffield				10.37		5./ 46				
Derby, Nottingham Road										
Derby	arr.	2.22	5.54	10.45	2./ 29	5./ 54	7./ 13	9./ 4	12.18	12.44

Above: Chesterfield, 1952. Taking on water on the down goods line is Beyer-Garratt No.47992. *E R Morten*

Below: Chesterfield, 1958. Not only is this a nice picture of a 'Crab' at work on its way south through the station with a train of sheeted wagons, but it also shows the MR signalling well. Approximately half a mile north and Tapton Junction is reached. This is the point of departure of the line to Sheffield from the 'Old Line'. On the fast line there are the standard signals for two block sections close together. For the slow lines, splitting distants are in use and just by the footbridge in the background are the corresponding home signals. *Midland Railway Trust*

List of places and customers served at Chesterfield, off the ex-Midland lines as shown in the Railway Clearing House 'Official Handbook of Railway Stations' 1938 edition

Station, sidings	Position
Boythorpe Lane Wharf	Brampton Branch
Brampton Brewery Co, siding	Brampton Branch
Brampton Wharf	Brampton Branch
British Furnaces Ltd	Chesterfield Tube Co siding
Bryan, Donkin & Co, siding	Chesterfield Tube Co siding
Chesterfield Corporation:	
Electric Lighting Depot	Brampton Branch
Gas Siding	Brampton Branch
Siding	J Pearson's London and Oldfield Potteries
Chesterfield & District Co-op , siding	Brampton Branch
Chesterfield Tube Co siding	Chesterfield
Clayton's Tannery	Near Chesterfield
Eastwood's Wagon Works	Near Chesterfield
Gibson & Co's siding	Near Chesterfield
Irving & Co	T Townrow's Siding
Lord's Mill Wharf	Near Chesterfield
Markham & Co Broad Oaks Iron Works	Chesterfield
Midland Co's Gas Works	Brampton Branch
J Pearson's London and Oldfield Potteries	Brampton Branch
Plowright Bros' siding	Brampton Branch
Robinson & Sons Goyt Side siding	J Pearson's London and Oldfield Potteries
Robinson & Sons Portland Works siding	Chesterfield
Saunder's Brick Works, Storforth Lane sidings	Near Chesterfield
Sheffield Pure Ice & Cold Storage Co siding	Brampton Wharf
Steel Breaking & Dismantling Co, Lockoford Siding	Near Chesterfield
T Townrow's Siding	Brampton Branch
J S Wilcockson Siding	Brampton Branch

Below: **Tapton Junction, 1961**. This is the site, just over half a mile north of Chesterfield, for the divergence of the 1870 line to Sheffield. Looking north from the footbridge shows Bristol Barrow Road's 'Patriot' class 4-6-0 No.45506 *The Royal Pioneer Corps* on the up fast line. Standing out on the sky line above the overbridge are the home signals for the junction. For the fast lines, the main route is the 'New Road' to Sheffield, while for the slow lines – the two on the right in this picture – it is the 'Old Road' through Eckington to Rotherham (Masborough). An example of a train which took *both* routes was the 2pm London St. Pancras to Bradford 'Yorkshire Express' run by the LMS in 1934. Having divided into two parts at Nottingham, the first went non-stop, taking the 'New Road' to Sheffield, then via Thornhill Junction, arriving at Bradford Exchange at 6.43pm. The second travelled along the 'Old Road', going on to Leeds and Bradford Forster Square station, getting there at 7.6pm.

The junction was the scene of a crash in 1906. A workman's train collided with a stationary engine just south of the Skull & Crossbones bridge. The wreckage was run into by a northbound goods train: several people were injured and there was one fatality. One engine involved was MR 0-6-0 No.1703.

Behind the trees on the right is Tapton House, described as a 'somewhat gloomy pile on the top of a hill', the last home of George Stephenson, who died there on 12 August 1848. *B Hoper*

CHESTERFIELD CENTRAL
61266

And finally...
Any account of Chesterfield must mention that there were three stations in the town, all belonging to different railway companies at one time. While the MR side has been dealt with, here are the other two.

Left, above: Chesterfield Central, 1951. This was the view looking north at Chesterfield Central station. Today it is part of the town's inner relief road. There was a short tunnel behind the photographer, just after the Infirmary Road bridge which carried the station entrance buildings and steps down to the two platforms. Most passenger trains on the Chesterfield loop were stoppers between Sheffield Victoria and Nottingham Victoria. Opened in 1892, by the Manchester, Sheffield & Lincolnshire Railway, the station become 'Central' in 1907 and closed in 1963. *Stations UK*

Left, below: Chesterfield Central, circa 1960. Hauling a local passenger train is LNER Class B1 4-6-0 No.61266. Shed code 41A was Darnell in Sheffield. At the northern end of the station the line went into a tunnel, emerging where the current main road does today. *Midland Railway Trust*

Above: Chesterfield Market Place, circa 1910. Opened as part of the grand scheme for the Lancashire, Derbyshire & East Coast Railway this was the largest station in the town. It boasted four platforms and had this fine building, which is still extant and in use today. When the Great Central Railway took control in 1907, it was distinguished from the company's other station, 'Central', by being named 'Market Place'. Problems with Bolsover tunnel caused the closure of this section of line to passengers in December 1951. *Stations UK*

Below: The gradient profile of the North Midland from Derby to Chesterfield shows how well the line stuck to easy grades.

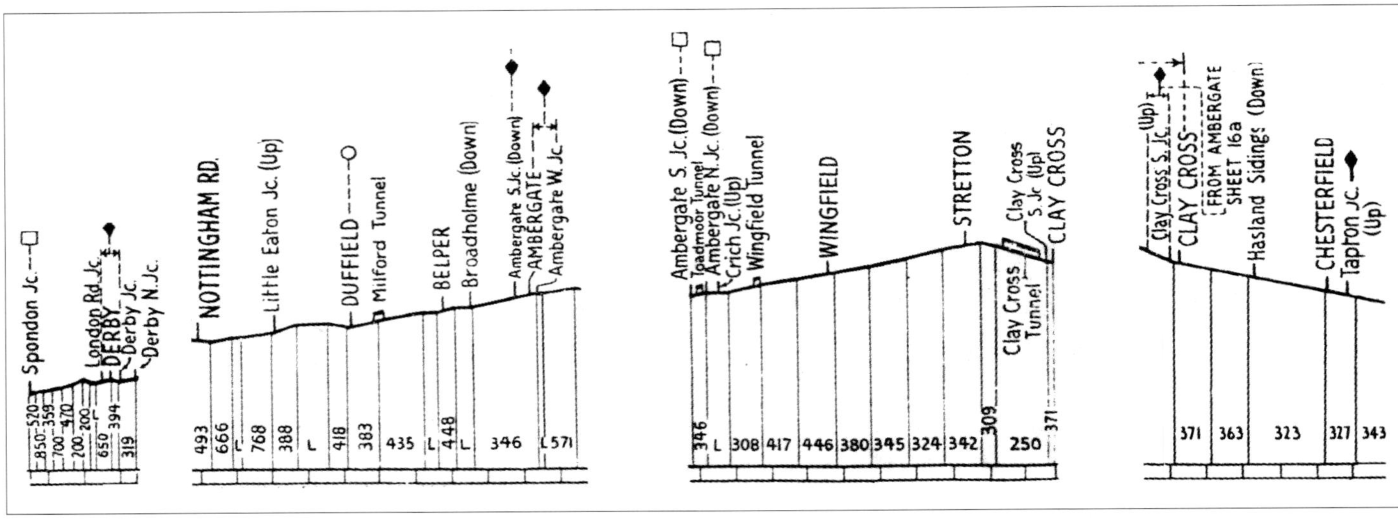

SPECIAL INSTRUCTIONS IN CONNECTION WITH CLAY CROSS TUNNEL:–

Communication with Signalmen.

Wires are provided, one on each wall of the tunnel, about six feet from the ground which, when cut or broken, give indication of this fact to the Signalman at the box at each end of the tunnel concerned. Where there are other wires, these special wires are always the lowest.

If for any reason the line is unsafe for the passage of trains, or a train is unable to proceed, or is divided, or if there is a serious personal injury, the following instructions must be observed:–

If the up line only is affected, the wire on the up side of the line must be cut or broken.
If the down line only is affected, the wire on the down side of the line must be cut or broken.
If both lines are affected, the wires on both the up and down sides of the line must be cut or broken.

Rear guard in case of train, and Fireman in case of light engine to break wire (or wires) as necessary. Lengthmen and Trainmen must not rely upon the cutting or breaking of the wires for the protection of the line or their trains, and these must be properly protected in accordance with Rules 178 to 180, or 217 as the case may be.

When the line is again clear the Signalman must be advised, and he must make an entry to this effect in the train register book, which must be signed by the person giving the advice.

Trains Divided

When this is done owing to the inability of the engine to haul the whole train the provisions of Rule 183 must be observed, except that when drawing a portion of the train out of the tunnel a lamp must be fixed at the rear of the last vehicle instead of a man riding on it.

Should a train be accidentally divided and the rear portion left in the tunnel, the Driver must not return on the same line for the portion left, but cross onto and travel along the proper line and recross at the signal box at the opposite end of the tunnel, and after obtaining Wrong Line Order form "D" from the Signalman, he must enter the tunnel and draw the rear portion of the train back to the box in rear, where the train must be run round and then proceed on its journey. The Driver must inform persons he passes when entering the tunnel that the train will return in the wrong direction.

When passing through the tunnel to get to the opposite end, the Driver must go slowly past the portion left in case anything might be foul of the road.

Ballast Train Working

When a ballast train is required to stop in this tunnel a Handsignalman must remain at the signal box in rear of the tunnel and protect the train with detonators and hand signals in accordance with the Rules.

When the work is completed and the train proceeds, it must be stopped at the signal box at the end of the tunnel, and the Guard must advise the Signalman that the work is complete and the line is clear, and when the Signalman has seen the tail lamp of the ballast train he must advise the Signalman at the box in rear that the Handsignalman may be withdrawn.